I0420829

Quote Octopus
Melbourne, Victoria, 3053
Australia
www.quoteoctopus.com

In many parts of the world, especially Pakistan and Afghanistan, terrorism, war and conflict stop children to go to their schools. We are really tired of these wars. Women and children are suffering.

Malala Yousafzai

Four years ago, I promised to end the war in Iraq. We did. I promised to refocus on the terrorists who actually attacked us on 9/11. We have. We've blunted the Taliban's momentum in Afghanistan, and in 2014, our longest war will be over. A new tower rises above the New York skyline, al Qaeda is on the path to defeat, and Osama bin Laden is dead.

Barack Obama

In his first term, President Barack Obama played a cautious manager navigating the worst economic disaster since the Great Depression and cleaning up the messes left by President George W. Bush in Iraq and Afghanistan.

Kevin O'Leary

When you're wounded and left on Afghanistan's plains, and the women come out to cut up what remains, jest roll to your rifle and blow out your brains and go to your gawd like a soldier.

Rudyard Kipling

People feel repressed by their own governments; they feel unfairly treated by the outside world; they wake up in the morning, and who do they see - they see people being shot and killed: all Muslims from Afghanistan, Iraq, Somalia, Sudan, Darfur.

Mohamed ElBaradei

President Obama has said that our aspirations should be realistic. We are not going to turn one of the poorest countries in the world, that was plunged into 30 years of war, into an advanced, industrialized, Western-style democracy. What we want to achieve is Afghanistan's capacity to secure and govern itself.

David Petraeus

It is not surprising that most Pakistanis do not support America's bombardment of Afghanistan. The Afghans are neighbours on the brink of starvation and devastated by war. America has shown itself to be untrustworthy, a superpower that uses its values as a scabbard for its sword.

Mohsin Hamid

The men and women of Afghanistan are building a nation that is free, and proud, and fighting terror - and America is honored to be their friend.

George W. Bush

Many soldiers returning from Iraq and Afghanistan suffer from serious, long-term, physical and mental health problems, due to their service. It is unconscionable to cut the already limited health care benefits available to these brave men and women.

Mark Dayton

When you decide to get involved in a military operation in a place like Syria, you've got to be prepared, as we learned from Iraq and Afghanistan, to become the government, and I'm not sure any country, either the United States or I don't hear of anyone else, who's willing to take on that responsibility.

Colin Powell

The young patriots now returning from war in Iraq and Afghanistan and other deployments worldwide are joining the ranks of veterans to whom America owes an immense debt of gratitude.

Steve Buyer

During the Cold War, America undertook serious military cuts only once: after the election of Richard Nixon, during the Vietnam War. The result: Vietnam fell to the Communists, the Russians moved into Afghanistan, and American influence around the globe waned dramatically.

Ben Shapiro

Most Pakistani politics is conducted within a narrow spectrum. Politicians spend much time debating the best ways to fight India, or take Kashmir, or dominate Afghanistan, or punish the United States for its real and imagined sins.

Stephen Kinzer

We've been in the nation-building business since World War I, and especially since WWII. The goal is not a Jeffersonian Democracy in Afghanistan, but a representative government that respects human rights, protects its own people, and is a friend of the West. These are very realistic - and necessary - goals.

Oliver North

Remember the rights of the savage, as we call him. Remember that the happiness of his humble home, remember that the sanctity of life in the hill villages of Afghanistan, among the winter snows, is as inviolable in the eye of Almighty God, as can be your own.

William E. Gladstone

'Bombing Afghanistan back into the Stone Age' was quite a favourite headline for some wobbly liberals. The slogan does all the work. But an instant's thought shows that Afghanistan is being, if anything, bombed out of the Stone Age.

Christopher Hitchens

The art of coalition command - whether it is here in Afghanistan, whether it was in Iraq or in Bosnia or in Haiti - is to take the resources you are provided with, understand what the strengths and weaknesses are and to employ them to the best overall effect.

David Petraeus

I am ready to sacrifice everything in completing the unfinished agenda of our noble jihad... until there is no bloodshed in Afghanistan and Islam becomes a way of life for our people.

Mohammed Omar

Operations in Iraq and Afghanistan and the war on terrorism have reduced the pace of military transformation and have revealed our lack of preparation for defensive and stability operations. This Administration has overextended our military.

Barack Obama

Pakistan is alarmed by the rising Indian influence in Afghanistan, and fears that an Afghanistan cleansed of the Taliban would be an Indian client state, thus sandwiching Pakistan between two hostile countries. The paranoia of Pakistan about India's supposed dark machinations should never be underestimated.

Salman Rushdie

I think we need to just be very clear about what we're trying to do in Afghanistan. Frankly, we're not trying to create the perfect democracy. We're never going to create some ideal society. We are simply there for our own national security.

David Cameron

I went to Afghanistan in '96 to write about terrorist training camps south of Jalalabad and Tora Bora, in the mountains. I was there right before the Taliban took over, literally a few weeks before they took Kabul. The frontline wasn't terribly active, but it was definitely there. And they swept into power.

Sebastian Junger

From the bitter cold winter at Valley Forge, to the mountains of Afghanistan and the deserts of Iraq, our soldiers have courageously answered when called, gone where ordered, and defended our nation with honor.

Solomon Ortiz

I'm finding myself really angry over spending and the deficit. I'm finding myself really angry over what's happening in the Middle East, the decision to stay in Afghanistan indefinitely. I'm angry about cap and trade. And I've been on record for a long time on the failed war on drugs.

Gary Johnson

I just think it would be unrealistic to suggest we're going to eliminate every last domestic insurgent in Afghanistan. Certainly, the history of the country would indicate that's not a very realistic objective, and I think we have to have realistic objectives.

Stephen Harper

The United States does not view our authority to use military force against Al Qaeda as being restricted solely to 'hot' battlefields like Afghanistan.

John O. Brennan

Winning in Afghanistan is having a country that is stable enough to ensure that there is no safe haven for Al Qaida or for a militant Taliban that welcomes Al Qaida. That's really the measure of success for the United States.

Leon Panetta

Canada is preparing to play a major role in the continued stability and security of Afghanistan through ISAF.

Paul Cellucci

Afghanistan is one of the poorest countries on earth. Security issue or no security issue, there would need to be a focus on it.

Helen Clark

Well Australia's been in Afghanistan from the get go, way back in 2001, but we have been resolute throughout and with support from both sides of Australian politics.

Kevin Rudd

In reality, Afghanistan has functioned as a nation-state for more than two centuries, and its army and bureaucracy reach back to the 19th century.

Gayle Tzemach Lemmon

No woman in Afghanistan is in business without support from either her husband or her father or her uncle, someone.

Gayle Tzemach Lemmon

The one thing you learn from looking at places like Afghanistan is that the power of business to do good is enormous.

Gayle Tzemach Lemmon

The United States will not be in Afghanistan forever.

Gayle Tzemach Lemmon

The women of Afghanistan have a voice, and it needs to be heard and not forgotten.

Gayle Tzemach Lemmon

I think of all the guys that strap a gun on their backs and head to Afghanistan and Iraq to keep us free and safe and maintain what America has stood for.

Foster Friess

I am now concerned with women's issues in a different way: women from Afghanistan, from Cambodia.

Emma Bonino

But I knew that what had happened was an eye-opener not only to the United States but also to Pakistan, who realized that after what has happened on the 11th of September, it was simply impossible to continue to play those games in Afghanistan.

Lakhdar Brahimi

But you are absolutely right that when the international community decides to help in a meaningful manner a country like Afghanistan, then coordination between the various actors that are involved in these processes is very, very difficult indeed.

Lakhdar Brahimi

Make no mistake, our troops will be in Afghanistan and Iraq for a long time.

Jerry Costello

People who need therapy are in Afghanistan. They've seen horrible human cruelty and degradation, but they don't have time or the money for therapy.

David Chase

In the 360-degree battlefields of Iraq and Afghanistan, women have served honorably and fought valiantly. Yet there is a key difference between being in harm's way and reacting to enemy contact, and being in a direct combat operations role day in and day out. They are different scenarios that require different standards.

Pete Hegseth

My time as editor has been overlapped by a crisis - a prolonged, labyrinthine, tragic, seemingly non-ending crisis - that involves the prehistory of 9/11, 9/11, Iraq, Afghanistan, fraught histories between the United States and almost everyone.

David Remnick

Especially right after 9/11. Especially when the war in Afghanistan is going on. There was a real sense that you don't get that critical of a government that's leading us in war time.

Walter Isaacson

I've always been fascinated with Navy SEALs in general and their role in Afghanistan in particular.

Christopher McQuarrie

Whether it's a kid in high school who doesn't have any friends and finds friends in my characters, or a guy in Afghanistan, who's trying to forget what he did that day, and trying not to think about what he's gotta do tomorrow... I give them a little bit of an escape.

R. A. Salvatore

We ought to recognize that we have an offensive responsibility to take the war to the terrorists where they are. That responsibility has waned in the last year as military and intelligence resources were withdrawn from Afghanistan and Pakistan to be used in Iraq.

Bob Graham

India has been contributing very much to the reconstruction of Afghanistan; we are strongly engaged there.

Joschka Fischer

Afghan society is very complex, and Afghanistan has a very complex culture. Part of the reason it has remained unknown is because of this complexity.

Mohsen Makhmalbaf

But also, there are no films being made about Afghanistan.

Mohsen Makhmalbaf

The Buddhas had to be destroyed by the Taliban to get the world thinking about Afghanistan.

Mohsen Makhmalbaf

We are not America. We are Afghanistan.

Hamid Karzai

I'm not good at explaining why I walked across Afghanistan.

Rory Stewart

Another part of the global war on terrorism that Canada and the United States are working on together is in helping failed states, states like Afghanistan, where people have no voice.

Paul Cellucci

The question in their minds was, why did the outside world, and particularly the Western world, produce all these landmines, and send them to Afghanistan? This business must be stopped. It's a dirty business to produce such a horrible device.

Mohsen Makhmalbaf

We must be honest in acknowledging that neither Germany nor the U.S. has the luxury of assuming that we can skate by on half-measures in Afghanistan and Pakistan and not risk suffering the consequences.

Susan Rice

In the British embassy in Afghanistan in 2008, an embassy of 350 people, there were only three people who could speak Dari, the main language of Afghanistan, at a decent level. And there was not a single Pashto speaker.

Rory Stewart

I think it's absolutely fascinating that in Berlin the parliament can discuss actively the role of their soldiers in Afghanistan because is it still possible, literally, for a German soldier to take up arms.

Stephen Daldry

In Afghanistan, life is so fragile; who knows what the next week will bring? That fragility really affects the way you're able to report, and the kind of stories people will tell you.

Gayle Tzemach Lemmon

When the Taliban captured Kabul in 1996 after a searing, four-year civil war, they immediately instituted laws which fit their utopic vision of the time of Islam's founding more than 1,300 years earlier. Afghan women's lives offered the most visible sign of the imagined past to which Afghanistan's present was to be returned.

Gayle Tzemach Lemmon

Americans worry that Afghanistan has become a petri dish in which the germs of Islamic fanaticism are replicating - soon Afghans will be hijacking American planes and bombing embassies everywhere. And their fears are not necessarily unfounded. The Taliban are unemployed war veterans, ready and even eager to return to the battlefield.

William T. Vollmann

I didn't vote for Bush, and I'm not happy particularly that he's president. But I will say I'm impressed that he didn't start bombing Afghanistan the day after Sept. 11. The more time that passes without him bombing Afghanistan, the more I respect him.

William T. Vollmann

The case of Afghanistan vs. the Soviet Union is the clearest case of good against evil that I've seen in my lifetime. I thought it was terrific the way they got their country back.

William T. Vollmann

The main thing that gives me hope is the media. We have radio, TV, magazines, and books, so we have the possibility of learning from societies that are remote from us, like Somalia. We turn on the TV and see what blew up in Iraq or we see conditions in Afghanistan.

Jared Diamond

When we look around the world today, when we see in Afghanistan that 10 million people have registered to vote in their upcoming elections, including 40 percent of those people are women, that's just unbelievable.

Laura Bush

The third point is that for some time the UN has been talking about helping Afghanistan in the reconstruction of the country but there has never been any real commitment by the international community to provide resources for that.

Lakhdar Brahimi

It is a fact that the Left routinely resists, then as now: Americans fought and died in Vietnam for freedom, just as they are doing in Iraq and Afghanistan today. Whatever mistakes generals and policymakers have made along the way cannot detract from that essential truth - which should be a part of any reliable history.

Arthur L. Herman

There is still a severe and scary amount of extreme poverty in rural parts of India, Pakistan, Afghanistan, Burma and sub-Saharan Africa.

Hans Rosling

Where's the progress that we're going to see in Afghanistan? You have to keep public support both on the economy and the war or these things will really become troubling.

Doris Kearns Goodwin

Last year I traveled to the Middle East to visit with troops in Kuwait, Iraq, and Afghanistan.

Kenny Marchant

The administration has a disturbing pattern of behavior when it comes to budgeting not only for the ongoing operations in Iraq and Afghanistan but also for military requirements not directly related to these conflicts.

Russ Feingold

My mission is to support our service members. They're volunteers, and if they're going to go to a hostile place like Afghanistan, I think we owe it to them to back them up and try to help them get through it.

Gary Sinise

Trauma is not the sole province of victims. If that were true, soldiers returning from Afghanistan wouldn't suffer from PTSD.

Jane Leavy

Losing their reproductive rights is the first step to how women live in Saudi Arabia and Afghanistan.

Patricia Richardson

Gen. Tommy Franks told me the war was being compromised as specialized personnel and equipment were being shifted from Afghanistan to prepare for the war in Iraq - a war more than a year away.

Bob Graham

I think we need to get the measurements that Congress has mandated from the White House on how we're going to determine progress in Afghanistan.

Jeanne Shaheen

Quite a few of the dogs that come back from Afghanistan or Iraq or police dogs that are involved in violent confrontations where there's gunfire can in fact exhibit the symptoms and suffer from PTSD.

Robert Crais

Romania will continue to fulfil its obligations in Afghanistan and Iraq.

Traian Basescu

There are tens of thousands of interactions every single day across Afghanistan between the Afghan troops and International Security Assistance Force. On most of those, every single day we continue to deepen and broaden the relationship we seek.

John R. Allen

'Each One Lost' I wrote the day after I got home. My week in Afghanistan was a very short trip, but it was a powerful experience.

Bruce Cockburn

We have to fight radical Islam wherever it exists. It's in Afghanistan, it's in Saudi Arabia, throughout the Middle-East in big numbers and it's in the United States.

Tom Tancredo

The war being fought in Afghanistan and Iraq is bringing about a fundamental change to the environment that has given rise and power to the extremists who export terrorism.

Craig L. Thomas

Do you know that every day, 10 people in Afghanistan are injured by landmines? It will continue for the next 50 years, because the country has the largest number of landmines in the world.

Mohsen Makhmalbaf

From my films, you can at least learn about Iran, you can get a sense of the history and the society. But no such films have been made about Afghanistan, so you really can't know much about it.

Mohsen Makhmalbaf

In Afghanistan, this is the problem, because everybody holds a piece of that mirror, and they all look at it and claim that they hold the entire truth.

Mohsen Makhmalbaf

A democratically elected congressman of the United States of America should not be talking of an ethnic divide in Afghanistan, should not be interfering in Afghanistan's internal affairs.

Hamid Karzai

General McChrystal had to go. Whatever his virtues as a strategist and commander, the 'Rolling Stone' interview fatally compromised his ability to represent the United States in dealing with allies and to act within the circle of people who must make decisions in Afghanistan.

Jim Talent

Given Mr. Obama's lack of experience as an executive, and his past performance in crises such as the oil spill, it is reasonable for those of us who support the effort in Afghanistan to worry that he will not be up to the job.

Jim Talent

I have not met, in Afghanistan, in even the most remote community, anybody who does not want a say in who governs them. Most remote community, I have never met a villager who does not want a vote.

Rory Stewart

We can't stay in Afghanistan forever.

James F. Amos

Look at Iraq; look at Afghanistan, where at great personal physical risk people have gone to the polls and have rejected the appeal from Bin Laden and his allies to stay at home.

Gijs de Vries

When al-Qaeda was on the run from Afghanistan crossing through Iran, some were arrested and they are imprisoned. Some of them are charged with some actions in Iran.

Akbar Hashemi Rafsanjani

We haven't been out in many of these countries helping them build infrastructure. How would they look at us today if we had been there helping them with some of that, rather than just being the people who are going to bomb in Iraq and go to Afghanistan?

Patty Murray

Over this August district work period, like many of my colleagues, I spent a lot of time with the men and women in uniform from my home State. The 196th Field Artillery Brigade just got back from a year in Afghanistan.

Zach Wamp

It was essentially for self defence that we went to war in Afghanistan and would go to war in Iraq.

Douglas Hurd

There is close to zero trust in institutions in Afghanistan. The mobile carriers have more trust than the banks.

Jan Chipchase

I think all of us who have been in Afghanistan on the ground multiple times know that what we're doing there on the ground is just not sustainable.

Bob Corker

Right now we're on the President Obama plan, and we'll stay with that. And from my perspective, the reason we're there is to make sure that we can achieve the principal goal which is ensure that Afghanistan can never become a safe haven for a terrorist organization like al Qaeda.

Michael Mullen

When I go there to Afghanistan or Pakistan, the question both asked - and if it's not asked, implied - is, 'Are you staying this time?' because we left last time, in 1989 in Afghanistan, and we sanctioned Pakistan from 1990 to 2002. So I think it's a fair question.

Michael Mullen

Instead, we did take our eye off the ball. We decided, instead of finishing the job in Afghanistan, to go into Iraq. And today, unfortunately, if you look at the situation on the ground, it is a mess.

Chris Van Hollen

Trying to rebuild Afghanistan on the cheap has left the country in the hands of warlords and an impotent Northern Alliance puppet regime that runs Kabul and nothing else.

Ted Rall

We can be proud of our record as an international beacon of liberty. From fostering democracies in Eastern Europe to the stabilization of Iraq and Afghanistan, we have been true to that calling and helped spread freedom to oppressed peoples everywhere.

Kay Bailey Hutchison

I'm a lucky boy! I could be holding a gun in Afghanistan. There's boys out there doing what they've got to do, and there's people digging holes, and there's people driving buses. And there's nothing wrong with that.

Ray Winstone

That's driven by any number of factors, the most prominent of which have been the combat experience of two major campaigns - one in Afghanistan and the other in Iraq - and the ongoing demands of the global war on terrorism.

Stephen Cambone

I think Americans understand that in Afghanistan, unlike in Iraq and Vietnam, we are fighting an enemy allied with the people who attacked us on 9/11.

Richard Holbrooke

We all know that, unfortunately, the media does not always portray the good things that are happening in Iraq and Afghanistan, and this will be a great opportunity for us to glean some information from the Iraqi women who are here for us to also take back to our constituents.

Ginny Brown-Waite

Kids coming back from Iraq and Afghanistan deserve to come back to 21st century medical care.

Anthony Principi

It's ironic that early on in the war with Afghanistan, the Americans and the British were saying, 'We recognise there must be a Palestinian state,' then they rapidly forgot about it. I think history will show that that kind of amnesia will come back to haunt you.

Tom Paulin

This is now a global war on terror and, indeed, it is important, it is imperative that we win in the battles in Afghanistan and that we win in the battles in Iraq. And as the gentleman from Georgia has mentioned, this is not something that is going to be quick and easy.

Marsha Blackburn

I oppose the spending of trillions in Iraq and Afghanistan, I strongly oppose Islamic extremism but don't believe that sending troops to die in two unwinnable wars makes sense.

Roger Stone

If we can't understand the Afghan family, we can't understand Afghanistan.

Asne Seierstad

Lasting peace and security in Iraq and Afghanistan will be achieved when we establish the conditions for democratic, economically viable nations.

John Warner

I think 2001 was the year Al Jazeera started to play an international role, in a way. Because in 2001, we were the only TV station located inside Kabul, and every image out of the war in Afghanistan, the beginning of the war in Afghanistan, came through Al Jazeera screen.

Wadah Khanfar

Many people in Britain will regard the end of combat in Afghanistan as a very good news story, but for many young men and women joining the Armed Forces, the lure of operations is a big recruiting sergeant, and we have to think how we are going to replace the excitement of operations for them with equally stimulating training and exercising.

Philip Hammond

Al Qaeda is on the run, partly because the United States is in Afghanistan, pushing on al Qaeda, and working internationally to cut off the flow of funds to al Qaeda. They are having a difficult time. They failed in this endeavor.

Ed Royce

But apart from the military measures, security measures, of course, Afghanistan needs great help for building up its social life, its economic life. It has become a very poor country, neglected for many years.

Bulent Ecevit

But if too many countries, as has been the case, interfere too much in the internal affairs, the political situation of Afghanistan, then of course we can't hope satisfactory results.

Bulent Ecevit

I suggested that we had experience in helping other countries build their military forces, and we would be willing and happy to do the same for Afghanistan, together with the United States.

Bulent Ecevit

A democratic and stable Iraq and Afghanistan are essential to our broader efforts to make no place safe for terrorists and to win the War on Terrorism.

Ben Nelson

If you want to understand what's happening to the situation in a town in Afghanistan, go down to the market. Is it vibrant? Is it safe? That will tell you an enormous amount about the security situation.

Gus O'Donnell

Afghanistan is going to be here a long time, and what's critical is that Afghanistan's relationship with its neighbors are, to the maximum extent they can be, constructive and operationally useful.

John R. Allen

And across Afghanistan, every single day, Afghan soldiers, Afghan police and ISAF troops are serving shoulder-to-shoulder in some very difficult situations. And our engagement with them, our shoulder-to-shoulder relationship with them, our conduct of operations with them every single day defines the real relationship.

John R. Allen

And the narrative for the Taliban that they can wait us out is a flawed narrative. I think that the unambiguous international support for Afghanistan has been a very powerful message. You know, that was the message that came out of the NATO summit. We will not abandon Afghanistan.

John R. Allen

There is a direct line relationship between what happened in Afghanistan in the work up to 11 September 2001 and what we're doing in Afghanistan today.

John R. Allen

Can that make any sense - a Belgian artist living in Mexico and working in Afghanistan?

Francis Alys

Stamps from Afghanistan are hilarious. You can tell when the revolutions are because suddenly they stop having pictures of the mullahs and the independence monument and they start having fish on them.

Samuel West

It's always a mistake for writers to key their submissions to world events, because they move so quickly and unpredictably, as has certainly proven the case in Afghanistan.

Richard Curtis

I'm the first girl from Afghanistan to lead a series in the United States.

Azita Ghanizada

Whenever my mom goes to Afghanistan, I'm just like, 'Bring me jewelry.'

Azita Ghanizada

There is no battle space the U.S. Military cannot access. They said we couldn't do Afghanistan. We did it with ease. They said we couldn't do Iraq. We did it with 150 combat casualties in six weeks. We did it so fast we weren't prepared for their collapse. There is nobody we can't take down. The question is, what do you do with the power?

Thomas P.M. Barnett

Even though the Bush campaign ad tells you that Afghanistan is a new democracy at the Olympics because of Bush's efforts, Afghanistan hasn't actually had an election.

Peter Schuyler

I'm also working with Mrs. Bush on some education projects in Afghanistan, so I get to see her a great deal.

Karen Hughes

In fact, if you look upon the situation today, there is great division in the world and we have failed to capitalize on that unity to finish the job in Afghanistan and against al Qaeda.

Chris Van Hollen

The president is being denounced for not taking the kind of pre-emptive action in Afghanistan that he has been so passionately denounced for taking in Iraq. Damned if he does and damned if he doesn't.

Ferdinand Mount

The true credit for our safety and security goes to our men and women who are serving in places like Iraq and Afghanistan in the global war on terrorism.

Asa Hutchinson

Like Afghanistan before it, Iraq is only one theater in a regional war. We were attacked by a network of terrorist organizations supported by several countries, of whom the most important were Iran, Iraq, Syria, and Saudi Arabia.

Michael Ledeen

I applaud President Obama's decision to begin a partial withdrawal of U.S. combat troops from Afghanistan. However, I believe that we must go further and have a full withdrawal of all U.S. combat troops.

Susan Bysiewicz

I come from a family of pacifists, so it's not like I was going to join the war. Sweden is not like the States or England where you might get sent to Afghanistan next month.

Bill Skarsgard

It seems not to matter that we are at the brink of a war that may spread beyond Afghanistan and Iraq to Iran and Georgia and then where? To Syria? To North Korea? To China? That we in America are in economic doldrums and are seeing small businesses fold and houses reclaimed by banks and a smouldering panic that is palpable everywhere.

Richard Schiff

There is a difference between a military mission and the aspiration for the long-term plans for the country. What we want is a stable enough Afghanistan, able to look after its own security so we can leave without the fear of it imploding... But let's be clear - it's not going to be perfect.

Liam Fox

We are not in Afghanistan for the sake of the education policy in a broken 13th-century country. We are there so the people of Britain and our global interests are not threatened.

Liam Fox

We can't afford to see Afghanistan roll backwards into a failed state that could become a base from which terrorist campaigns can be launched anywhere in the world.

Liam Fox

Certainly the existence of these huge nuclear force was important for the ultimate confrontation, let's say, over western Europe. You just can't use them to deal with a situation like Afghanistan.

Lloyd Cutler

In 1979, when I was toddler, the Russians invaded Afghanistan, and my whole family fled to Vienna, Virginia. Far from home, my parents were determined to raise my two sisters and me according to Afghan traditions.

Azita Ghanizada

Secret ops by secret forces have a nasty tendency to produce unintended, unforeseen, and completely disastrous consequences. New Yorkers will remember well the end result of clandestine U.S. support for Islamic militants against the Soviet Union in Afghanistan during the 1980s: 9/11.

Nick Turse

Eighty-five percent cannot read when they enter the security forces of Afghanistan. Why? Because the Taliban withheld education during the period of time in which these men and women would have learned to read.

James G. Stavridis

Britain, along with the U.S.A., is war weary, and after the travesty of Iraq and Afghanistan, has grave misgivings in any future involvement in the Middle East. The ghost of Tony Blair and his single-minded determination to attack Iraq, at any cost, has cast a long shadow over British politics. The British public have a long collective memory.

Paul Conroy

I can't say enough about the tremendous work the Missouri National Guard has done as part of our military efforts in Afghanistan, Iraq and other countries.

Jay Nixon

President Obama had voiced strong support for the effort in Afghanistan during his campaign, pledging to add two brigades, which he did. But since the inauguration... the administration had signaled that the U.S. commitment needed careful assessment, and we needed to recalibrate the strategy and objectives.

Stanley A. McChrystal

In my 20 years as a photographer, covering conflicts from Bosnia to Gaza to Iraq to Afghanistan, injured civilians and soldiers have passed through my life many times.

Anja Niedringhaus

Afghanistan remains an opportunity to deal al Qaeda a vital strategic blow, especially since we have abandoned all operations - including counterterrorism operations - in Iraq.

Jack Keane

The Taliban has not, in my judgment, in any significant way changed their fundamental goal and objective, which is to take over Afghanistan and return to running that country. It doesn't mean that we shouldn't have negotiation talks with them. I think we should. But we've got to be clear-eyed about it.

Jack Keane

I understand why so many Americans were angry when I was first discovered in Afghanistan. I realize many still are, but I hope in time that feeling will change.

John Walker Lindh

I was distressed that after 9/11, when the United States was attacked by terrorists, the United States' response was to attack Afghanistan, where some of the terrorists had been.

Alice Walker

If American forces leave Afghanistan, the Taliban is going to do what to America? Don't say you're worried about what they will do to the Afghan people. If that was America's concern, America's operational presence there would be much different.

Henry Rollins

I believe in the transformational power of liberty. I believe that the free Iraq is in this nation's interests. I believe a free Afghanistan is in this nation's interest.

George W. Bush

In Afghanistan, there is a plan to build democracy; hundreds of thousands of troops are protecting it. There is a plan to rebuild and reconstruct there. But many thousands of Americans die from violence and poverty every year and we don't have a plan for reconstruction at home.

Jesse Jackson

You go to London, you see a TV set in every cell and the sign up that all the officers must treat prisoners with dignity. What about your dedicated soldiers that have helped fight in Afghanistan and Iraq? They're living in tents and our soldiers are living in tents. So it's OK for soldiers to live in tents, in hot tents, but it's wrong for inmates?

Joe Arpaio

What President Bush did in his doctrine of preemptive strike and in his war in Afghanistan and in Iraq was to turn even his allies in Europe negatively toward America.

Louis Farrakhan

For me, it's an honor for the military to ask me to go to Iraq, Afghanistan, or GITMO. I'm happy to go.

R. Lee Ermey

Never underestimate the ability of political leaders to misread history on a monumental scale. The invasions of Iraq and Afghanistan have both served to hasten western decline: they have both failed to achieve their objectives and in the process demonstrated an underlying western impotence.

Martin Jacques

I taught high school for one year in Deerfield Beach, Fla., and in the end, it was such an enjoyable experience breaking up fights daily, that I decided to return to the combat zone of Afghanistan.

Allen West

In Afghanistan, you don't understand yourself solely as an individual. You understand yourself as a son, a brother, a cousin to somebody, an uncle to somebody. You are part of something bigger than yourself.

Khaled Hosseini

When I go to Afghanistan, I realize I've been spared, due to a random genetic lottery, by being born to people who had the means to get out. Every time I go to Afghanistan I am haunted by that.

Khaled Hosseini

We have to have a conversation about whether Obama's plan to increase spending to occupy Afghanistan helps make America a safer country, or not. I think at some point, we may decide that we don't have to have that size military and cost footprint in the country. You look at what you want to accomplish, how many soldiers you need.

Grover Norquist

There's no doubt that it's still a dangerous place, Afghanistan. The fortunate thing is that the United States was helping to provide security for Chairman Karzai. And it shows that the United States is committed to that regime.

Condoleezza Rice

Working with kids in Soweto in South Africa, it's rough out there. But the bottom line is you've got to go to know. In Cambodia, there are 10,000 landmines. Same in Afghanistan, same in Colombia. I'm totally addicted to traveling.

Quincy Jones

We can stay in Afghanistan and stabilize the situation, or we can get out and win, or we can get out and lose.

Dinesh D'Souza

Afghanistan is a rural nation, where 85 percent of people live in the countryside. And out there it's very, very conservative, very tribal - almost medieval.

Khaled Hosseini

As the daughter of a 25-year veteran of the armed forces, I am incredibly thankful for the sacrifices our women and men have made in Iraq, and continue to make in Afghanistan.

Barbara Lee

People in Afghanistan want peace, including the Taliban.
They're also people like we all are. They have families, they
have relatives, they have children, they are suffering a tough
time.

Hamid Karzai

I feel most empires fell when they started to act human, but
then look at Russia. They kept a pretty strong hand, and they
fell from Afghanistan alone because Afghanistan is the
graveyard of empires. I guess you just can't sustain it.

Colin Quinn

A fly cannot go in unless it stops somewhere; therefore
weapons, fuel, food, money will not go to Afghanistan unless
the neighbors of Afghanistan are working, are cooperating,
either being themselves the origin or the transit.

Lakhdar Brahimi

Afghanistan is a country in need. Afghanistan needs to protect
itself in the region; Afghanistan needs to secure itself within
the country. Afghanistan needs to develop its forces, and
Afghanistan needs to provide stability to the people.

Hamid Karzai

Afghanistan is very satisfied with Croatia's participation in the NATO-led peace mission and expects Croatia to expand its contribution to peace restoration in Afghanistan to other areas as well.

Hamid Karzai

I always get very fit if I'm going away filming for two months in Afghanistan or wherever.

Ross Kemp

It is in line with the fundamental interests of the two peoples for China and Afghanistan to strengthen a strategic and cooperative partnership, which is also conducive to regional peace, stability and development.

Zhou Yongkang

They're criminals, they brutalized Afghanistan, they killed our people, they destroyed our land.

Hamid Karzai

We as the Afghan people and government are willing to help Pakistan work for peace in Afghanistan and work for peace in Pakistan, together.

Hamid Karzai

I believe that everyone can appreciate the right of a family to grieve the loss of a loved one in peace, regardless of anyone's position on the war in Iraq and Afghanistan.

Dave Reichert

As for the United States' future in Afghanistan, it will be fire and hell and total defeat, God willing, as it was for their predecessors - the Soviets and, before them, the British.

Mohammed Omar

A day in Afghanistan is like a week at home.

Ross Kemp

As an infantry officer who served in Iraq, Afghanistan, and Guantanamo Bay, I have led men in combat and trained them on tactics and strategy. The mission of the infantry is to 'close with, and destroy, the enemy.' Our job, in a direct way, is to fight and win wars.

Pete Hegseth

It is no secret that many Islamic movements in the Middle East tend to be authoritarian, and some of the so-called 'Islamic regimes' such as Saudi Arabia, Iran - and the worst case was the Taliban in Afghanistan - they are pretty authoritarian. No doubt about that.

Mustafa Akyol

I have never believed you go to war in Iraq, you go to war in Afghanistan, and believe that you can deal with those battlefields, those countries, in microcosms, or narrow channels.

Chuck Hagel

Women in Afghanistan do not ask the United States to stay for the simple or sentimental reason of safeguarding their rights. They are the first ones to say that this is not enough of a reason for the world's remaining superpower to remain in their country.

Gayle Tzemach Lemmon

We don't consider the battle has ended in Afghanistan... The battle has begun and its fires are picking up. These fires will reach the White House, because it is the center of injustice and tyranny.

Mohammed Omar

The mission - the overall mission is to dismantle and defeat and disrupt al-Qaeda. But we have to make sure there's not a safe haven that returns in Afghanistan.

Michael Mullen

Since 2001, people have been scared. There's been some really scary stuff that's been happening - 9/11, Iraq, Afghanistan, Katrina, anthrax letters, D.C. sniper, global warming, global financial meltdown, bird flu, swine flu, SARS. I think people really feel like the system's breaking down.

Max Brooks

You would have thought that after 9/11 the president would have finished the job in Afghanistan, and kept the focus on capturing Bin Laden and his al-Qaeda deputies, but he and his team gave top priority to their original plan to invade Iraq.

Bill Nelson

We don't see that the Taliban ultimately can succeed, and it's a combination both of what the international community can do to support Afghanistan, not just in the short term, but over the long term.

John R. Allen

Nevertheless, I do know that we are part of a danger zone, we have military operations in Afghanistan and we're training the Iraqi police force. The terrorists also have us in their sights.

Otto Schily

In places like South Afghanistan, where cultural norms prevent men from entering homes, female vaccinators often make the difference between a closed or opened door.

Ksenia Solo

WikiLeaks exposed corruption, war crimes, torture and cover-ups. It showed that we were lied to about the wars in Iraq and Afghanistan; that the U.S. military had deliberately hidden information about systematic torture and civilian casualties, which were much higher than reported.

Jemima Khan

The experts who managed the original Marshall Plan say Afghanistan needs a commitment of at least $5 to $10 billion over 5 to 10 years, coupled with occupation forces of 250,000 Allied soldiers to keep the peace throughout the country.

Ted Rall

An interim government was set up in Afghanistan. It included two women, one of whom was Minister of Women's Affairs. Man, who'd she have to show here ankles to to get that job?

Tina Fey

Clinton has more important things to worry about. He not only risks being destroyed historically, like Afghanistan's Buddha statues; he also could end up going to jail.

Ed Koch

We didn't do anything wrong, but among the lessons learned, given the magnitude of the problems we now face in Afghanistan, a major U.S. force on the ground would convince the world we were in for the long-haul recovery of a country devastated by 21 years of warfare.

Alexander Haig

The big nest was in Afghanistan, thats not quite cleared, then there are nests in the Philippines, there are nests in Indonesia, the Malaysians are clearing up their nests.

Lee Kuan Yew

What's always got me is the fact that when people talked on the telly about Iraq, before Afghanistan kicked off, you'd get only these public-school-type army officers talking about what was going on out there. I kept thinking, 'Why don't we get the true voice of the squaddie? Why don't we hear from the lads on the battlefield?'

Ross Kemp

You know, I agree with President Obama that in Iraq and Afghanistan, at some point in time, we have to take the training wheels off and we have to allow those countries to stand on their own two feet.

Josh Mandel

After 2014, we will support a unified Afghanistan as it takes responsibility for its own future.

Barack Obama

America's foreign policy lacks the backbone to do the right thing in Afghanistan - which is leave.

Henry Rollins

I want the troops from Great Britain and the U.S. to be successful, but by the same token, Afghanistan has always been a screw-up.

Clint Eastwood

It is very clear that the people in Afghanistan do not want the Taliban back.

Hillary Clinton

Now, I know there are many Americans who say, 'Get out of Afghanistan. Bring 'em all home.' And there are others who say, 'Put in hundreds of thousands of more.'

Hillary Clinton

I mean Afghanistan is a very rugged, complicated country.

Barbara Bush

Our presence in Afghanistan is not worth the price of any more American lives or treasure.

Camille Paglia

In the 1980s America reacted to the Soviet Union's invasion of Afghanistan. We supported a war that left a nation torn to pieces. And as the last Soviet tank left the country, so did we.

Simon Sinek

I thanked President Obama for the United States' work in supporting education in Pakistan and Afghanistan and for Syrian refugees.

Malala Yousafzai

The world starts to exist, for Americans, when we are in conflict with a place. And then all of a sudden, Afghanistan pops up on the TV screen and it becomes a place. And it exists for three weeks, and then it disappears into thin air.

Isabel Allende

I have a very deep concern about President Obama putting in another 21,000 troops into Afghanistan with the promise of more to come.

George McGovern

Now I'm doing a film festival for kids and writing a script about a kidnapped journalist in Afghanistan.

Olivia Wilde

No one talked about the fact that in this year under the Obama administration you've seen the highest casualties in Afghanistan. And the fact that it took him almost 90 days to figure out what his strategy is going to be was absolutely appalling.

Allen West

My go-to gifts are scarves from my friend Matin Maulawizada's nonprofit organization, Afghan Hands, which supports disenfranchised women in Afghanistan. In exchange for their beautiful embroidery, the women are given financial aid and classes in math and literacy. The scarves are all stunning and one of a kind.

Claire Danes

I try to get over to Iraq and Afghanistan as much as I can.

R. Lee Ermey

During the 19th century, Britain fought two wars in unsuccessful attempts to subjugate the Afghans. When Britain finally drew a border between India and Afghanistan in 1893, Pashtun tribes in southern Afghanistan were cut off from related tribes across the border in what was then India and is now Pakistan.

Stephen Kinzer

If Iraq and Afghanistan have taught us anything in recent history, it is the unpredictability of war and that these things are easier to get into than to get out of, and, frankly, the facile way in which too many people talk about, 'Well, let's just go attack them.'

Robert M. Gates

You know what I had a problem with? The war - the war in Afghanistan.

Lupe Fiasco

And the fact of the matter is there were thousands of people that went through those training camps in Afghanistan. We know they are seeking deadlier weapons - chemical, biological and nuclear weapons if they can get it.

Dick Cheney

Since the attack on the United States on September 11 2001, and the US retaliation in Afghanistan and Iraq, there must be few people who have not felt a twinge of nostalgia for the cold war.

James Buchan

Fiction is a very powerful tool for teaching history. The Philippines was the first Iraq, the first Vietnam, the first Afghanistan, in the sense that it was the United States' initial or baptismal experience in nation-building.

Miguel Syjuco

Since the intervention in Afghanistan, we suddenly began to notice when, in political discussions, we found ourselves only among Europeans or Israelis.

Jurgen Habermas

Afghanistan has moved forward and Afghanistan will defend itself. And the progress that we have achieved, the Afghan people will not allow it to be put back or reversed.

Hamid Karzai

Don't kid yourself. President Obama's decision to withdraw 33,000 troops from Afghanistan before he stands for reelection is not driven by the United States' 'position of strength' in the war zone as much as it is by grim economic and political realities at home.

Ron Fournier

It's a tribal state, and it always will be. Whether we like it or not, whenever we withdraw from Afghanistan, whether it's now or years from now, we'll have an incendiary situation. Should we stay and play traffic cop? I don't think that serves our strategic interests.

Jon Huntsman, Jr.

From 2002 to the end of his presidency, George W. Bush routinely was accused by the Left of 'creating chaos:' chaos in Iraq, chaos in Afghanistan, chaos in the Muslim world, chaos among our allies.

Monica Crowley

Now, al Qaeda's on the run. Afghanistan is no longer a base of operations. The Afghan government is a friendly government that is trying to bring democracy to its people.

Condoleezza Rice

Barack Obama's life was so much simpler in 2009. Back then, he had refined the cold act of blaming others for the bad economy into an art form. Deficits? Blame Bush's tax cuts. Spending? Blame the wars in Iraq and Afghanistan. No business investment? Blame Wall Street.

John Sununu

I think the emancipation of women in Afghanistan has to come from inside, through Afghans themselves, gradually, over time.

Khaled Hosseini

If the United States is treating Afghanistan as a sovereign country it has to prove it.

Hamid Karzai

A military or government hierarchy is anathema to the dispersed population and diverse tribes of mountainous Afghanistan.

Iqbal Quadir

The events of September 11 and what has happened since have made people understand that even a small, distant and far away country like Afghanistan cannot be left to break up into anarchy and chaos without consequences for the whole world.

Lakhdar Brahimi

The attacks of 9/11 came out of Afghanistan. It was a failed state, a rogue nation. That's why al Qaeda was there in the first place.

Sebastian Junger

Whether you are a stay-at-home mum, or on the red carpet, or in Afghanistan, the better you feel, the better you do your job.

Bobbi Brown

I had earlier concluded that a war with Iraq would be a distraction from the successful and expeditious completion of our aims in Afghanistan. Now I had come to question whether the White House was telling the truth.

Bob Graham

I am always revolted when Islamic leaders, from Afghanistan or elsewhere, deny the very existence of female oppression, avoid the issue by pointing to examples of what they view as Western mistreatment of women, or even worse, justify the oppression of women on the basis of notions derived from Sharia law.

Khaled Hosseini

Ultimately, my books are not about the politics, although the toil and the struggle and the wars in Afghanistan have a significant impact on the lives of my characters.

Khaled Hosseini

As far as Iraq, the important thing is that the Taliban is gone in Afghanistan, three-quarters of the al-Qaida leadership is either dead or in jail, and we now have Saudi Arabia working with us, Pakistan working with us.

Peter T. King

The misery in war-torn Afghanistan is reminiscent of images from the Thirty Years' War.

Jurgen Habermas

Afghanistan must never again be a safe haven for terrorism.

Julia Gillard

As the president of Afghanistan I look at the suffering of our people as a whole.

Hamid Karzai

I don't think the Taliban will ever come back to take Afghanistan, no.

Hamid Karzai

The legal system in Afghanistan is very immature and porous.

Lindsey Graham

The United States can't impose democracies. We can't impose our will. The Russians found that out in Afghanistan.

Chuck Hagel

Obama is thoroughly mixed up with all these things he's got. He's got to solve Libya. He's got to solve Afghanistan. He's everywhere. And this nation, I don't know why it's not showing the leadership and capacity to attend different issues at the same time.

Vicente Fox

We're here so that Afghanistan does not once again become a sanctuary for transnational extremists the way it was when al-Qaeda planned the 9/11 attacks in the Kandahar area, conducted the initial training for the attackers in training camps in Afghanistan before they moved on to Germany and then to U.S. flight schools.

David Petraeus

Let us also reflect on the honorable service of our men and women of the U.S. Armed Forces currently serving our country overseas in Iraq and Afghanistan, and around the world.

John Linder

The big risk to British lives in 2013 is in Afghanistan. Our troops, diplomats and aid workers have made a big contribution there. But while there is an end date for Western engagement, 2014, there isn't a proper end game.

David Miliband

Well, first, the situation in Afghanistan is much better than it was. But there is no comparison between Afghanistan and Iraq. Iraq has a bureaucracy, Iraq has wealth. Iraq has an educated class of people who are positioned to come in and take over.

Peter T. King

I do dream about Afghanistan. I wake up and think I'm still there.

Ross Kemp

According to the official version of history, CIA aid to the Mujahadeen began during 1980, that is to say, after the Soviet army invaded Afghanistan, 24 Dec 1979.

Zbigniew Brzezinski

Obama is making a choice now that will lead to the deaths of many thousands of civilians in Afghanistan by American hands. By ordinary standards of presidents, he is a decent man. But those standards aren't good enough. He's in a position either to kill or not to kill, and he's made the decision to kill.

Daniel Ellsberg

No one argues that we should have imposed a dictatorship in Afghanistan having liberated the country. Similarly, we weren't about to impose a dictatorship in Iraq having liberated the country.

Paul Wolfowitz

The first thing to recognize not just about Afghanistan but about any poor undeveloped country is that as big as it looks on the map, it's much bigger when you're there.

Robert D. Kaplan

There's an 800 kilometer border between Iran and Afghanistan.

Mohsen Makhmalbaf

As we continue to make great progress in the war on terror, now more than ever, it is important that members of the international community stand-by and bolster the efforts of the emerging diplomatic leaders in Iraq and Afghanistan.

James Inhofe

The military alone cannot end the conflict in Afghanistan. On that much nearly everyone can agree, offering a rare island of consensus among sides otherwise divided on the question of how and when America's longest-ever war should wind down.

Gayle Tzemach Lemmon

Since January 2002, when the United States began detaining at Guantanamo Bay enemy combatants captured in Afghanistan, Iraq, and other fronts in the war on terror, critics have complained of human rights abuses.

Linda Chavez

As you know, I did not support the United States' engagement in Iraq and have long had concerns about Afghanistan... But I obviously have always been 100 percent supportive of our military.

Kyrsten Sinema

With the winding down of the conflicts in Iraq and Afghanistan, the United States now has an opportunity to implement real defense reforms without having a serious impact on immediate battlefield needs.

Pete Hegseth

The rapid proliferation of cell phones in Afghanistan proves that anything that adds value to people's lives spreads like brushfire - and commerce is certainly a force that could add value for Afghanis.

Iqbal Quadir

Ataturk sent several Turkish staff officers to Afghanistan, helped them build their own army.

Bulent Ecevit

The West has been able to bring Afghanistan a much better health service, better education, better roads, a better economy, though some have benefited more; some have benefited less from that economic well-being in Afghanistan.

Hamid Karzai

Perhaps we underestimated the challenges in Afghanistan in the past. That's why we are now strengthening and intensifying our commitment.

Anders Fogh Rasmussen

You could get a cheer by saying: 'Let's withdraw from Afghanistan', but I don't think that's where the public's at. It wouldn't be responsible.

Ed Balls

We are so appreciative of the men and women in uniform who are protecting us, whether in Afghanistan or Iraq or on ships around the world. For our security, they are taking the offensive to the terrorists overseas.

George Allen

The terrorist attacks of September 11th and the courageous actions of our armed forces in Afghanistan and Iraq remind us that friends of tyranny and enemies of freedom still exist.

Carl Levin

I think the central mission in Afghanistan right now is to protect the people, certainly, and that would be inclusive of everybody, and that in a, in an insurgency and a counterinsurgency, that's really the center of gravity.

Michael Mullen

One of the lessons of Vietnam, which we failed to heed in the Iraq war and the Afghanistan surge, is that before you commit

U.S. military forces to aid or assist, it is essential to know what you want them to achieve.

Kathleen Troia McFarland

It's an amazing thing to hear they're finally giving out a Medal of Honor to a soldier from the wars of Iraq and Afghanistan.

Tim Hetherington

If today is anything like the typical day of the past 3 years, three American soldiers will die in Iraq or Afghanistan, the Taliban will get a little stronger in Afghanistan and the civil war will continue to be enhanced in Iraq.

Alcee Hastings

You could say that bad typography brought us the Afghanistan war, the Iraq war, the housing crisis and a good number of other things.

Stefan Sagmeister

Our neighbor Canada has 2,200 troops serving in Afghanistan. Canada has also assumed responsibility for the Provincial Reconstruction Team in Kandahar, which was originally established by our own military.

Tom Lantos

We have been helping, trying to help Afghanistan in many ways, even from the beginning of... the beginnings of the '20s, 1920s, when he we were fighting our own national struggle.

Bulent Ecevit

Failure in Afghanistan would have profound consequences for our national security. It would undermine the NATO alliance structure that has been the bedrock of Britain's defence for the last 60 years... I will not allow this to happen on my watch.

Bob Ainsworth

We don't want the Taliban to put down roots, or the al Qaeda to put down roots in Afghanistan that can facilitate Afghanistan becoming - once again - a launching pad for international terrorism.

John R. Allen

We're pursuing a strategic partnership with Afghanistan on the case of the United States and Afghanistan where we're going to push toward a future. It is the future that the Afghans desire with the United States. It is a future that the Afghans desire with the international community and we desire that as well.

John R. Allen

As we begin to leave Afghanistan, are we fooling ourselves about what we are leaving behind or what we have promised the people of Afghanistan? Especially the women and girls?

Greta Van Susteren

It is the responsibility of Afghanistan's new government to gain better control over the country's administration and to resolutely fight the drug trade and corruption.

Anders Fogh Rasmussen

We can no longer apply the classic criteria to clearly determine whether and when we should use military force. We are waging war in Afghanistan, for example, but it's an asymmetrical war where the enemies are criminals instead of soldiers.

Otto Schily

Carter's hopes died when the Soviet Union invaded Afghanistan and he ended up having to reverse policy and launch the military buildup that Reagan continued. Mr. Obama would be forced back into a war on terror if terrorist groups pull off enough damaging or frightening attacks to force this issue to the fore.

Walter Russell Mead

I decided in '96 to dedicate my life to mostly promoting literacy and education for girls in rural Pakistan and Afghanistan.

Greg Mortenson

America has survived and grown stronger through September 11th and subsequent wars with Afghanistan and Iraq and those who seek to do us harm. We have faced - and met - tremendous challenges ramping up a public health and safety system to protect Americans from future threats.

Christopher Bond

Some have called Afghanistan 'the graveyard of empires,' and it probably is the graveyard of empires.

James G. Stavridis

The brave and capable women who served in Iraq and Afghanistan have performed admirably.

Susan Davis

The fate of Syria hangs in the balance, but it is entirely possible that the fall of the Assad regime will result in anarchy and cause Syria to turn into a second Afghanistan, a base for anti-Israel terrorism.

Martin Van Creveld

A simple leather jacket... has gotten me through cocktail parties in New York and cold nights in Afghanistan.

Ronan Farrow

We in the West walked away from Afghanistan at the end of the Cold War and left it as a country devastated socially and armed to the teeth. If we do that again, there will be consequences.

Bob Ainsworth

The British soldiers serving in Afghanistan alongside Prince Harry were in exceptional danger until he was withdrawn.

John Eisenhower

Whether I'm trying to figure out what the U.S. military is doing in Latin America or Africa, Afghanistan or Qatar, the response is remarkably uniform - obstruction and obfuscation, hurdles and hindrances. In short, the good old-fashioned military runaround.

Nick Turse

A trillion dollars spent, 2,000 American lives lost - Afghanistan is the longest war in American history. But you don't hear a word about it.

Michael Baumgartner

I want the American people to understand, we have a clear and focused goal: to disrupt, dismantle and defeat Al Qaeda in Pakistan and Afghanistan.

Stanley A. McChrystal

We're in danger of breaking our army and preventing our national leaders from having the flexibility to confront not just Iraq and Afghanistan, but crises around the globe.

Jack Reed

In June 2010, after more than 38 years in uniform, in the midst of commanding a 46-nation coalition in a complex war in Afghanistan, my world changed suddenly - and profoundly. An article in 'Rolling Stone' magazine depicting me, and people I admired, in a manner that felt as unfamiliar as it was unfair, ignited a firestorm.

Stanley A. McChrystal

The most successful cultural diplomacy strategy integrates people-to-people or arts/culture/media-to-people interactions into the basic business of diplomacy. The programs in Afghanistan, Egypt, and Iran all contribute to core goals of U.S. policy in those countries.

Cynthia P. Schneider

We've been at war for 10 years with this generation of Marines. We've seen women do a whole lot of things between the war in Iraq and the current war in Afghanistan. The fact that I'm sitting here making sure that we continue to put out the best young Marines is just a matter of it being 2011.

Loretta Reynolds

Afghanistan is where much of the al Qaeda journey began. It is the main site where Osama bin Laden, Mullah Omar and their cohort rose to prominence fighting the Soviets in the 1980s. Afghan territory holds special significance to the group, which is committed to retaking it and re-establishing it as the base of a global movement.

Jack Keane

We cannot continue to ask the brave men and women of our Armed Forces to put their lives on the line to protect our country while we jeopardize their safety by failing to ensure that Defense Department funds are not siphoned off to warlords in Afghanistan.

John F. Tierney

For too many families, the aftershock of the war in Afghanistan will be felt every day, most probably for the rest of their lives. I know because I've looked into the eyes and the faces of grieving mothers.

Ross Kemp

When an army unit returns from service in Iraq or Afghanistan, it barely gets a breather before it begins training for its next deployment.

Hillary Clinton

I don't think the war in Afghanistan was ruthlessly enough waged.

Christopher Hitchens

I'm saying 9/11 was to get us into Iraq and get us into Afghanistan.

Jesse Ventura

It matters not what your individual position is on either war we are currently prosecuting - in Iraq or Afghanistan - certainly we can all agree protesting at military funerals is a cruel and unnecessary hardship on our military families during their most difficult hour.

Solomon Ortiz

I also know that there are a lot of people around the United States who want my husband to win and who are for him and who support our troops in Iraq and Afghanistan. And I feel good about those people, too.

Laura Bush

I have defended the interests of France at the G8 in Washington; afterwards I was at Chicago to announce the withdrawal of French troops from Afghanistan; I have participated in two European summits, so I have fully respected the engagements I made to the French.

Francois Hollande

If there's ever an example that military power alone cannot be successful in Afghanistan, I think it was the Soviet experience.

Robert M. Gates

Cults, or related social movements such as the Taliban in Afghanistan, result in massive military expenses.

Keith Henson

We did not go to war in Afghanistan or in Iraq to, quote, 'impose democracy.' We went to war in both places because we saw those regimes as a threat to the United States.

Paul Wolfowitz

The problem in Afghanistan is really not so much land as water. It's a dry country with ample amounts of water running through it, but not to good enough effect.

P. J. O'Rourke

The war on terror is the war in Afghanistan.

Nancy Pelosi

Most liberals I know were for invading Afghanistan right after 9/11.

Michael Moore

How could a guy sitting in a cave in Afghanistan, have... plotted so perfectly the hijacking of four planes and then guaranteed that three of them would end up precisely on their targets?

Michael Moore

As someone who's spent time with our troops in Iraq and Afghanistan on USO tours and met wounded warriors at Walter Reed and Bethesda, I feel a deep obligation to the men and women who have risked life and limb on our behalf.

Al Franken

Military hardliners called me a 'security threat' for promoting peace in South Asia and for supporting a broad-based government in Afghanistan.

Benazir Bhutto

Anyone who's traveled with me to Afghanistan knows why I love this book: 'War,' by Sebastian Junger.

Joe Biden

I know now that what countries do at summits has the power to help girls in Pakistan, Nigeria or Afghanistan.

Malala Yousafzai

Al Qaeda is almost all in Pakistan, and Pakistan has nuclear weapons. And yet for every dollar we're spending in Pakistan, we're spending $30 in Afghanistan. Does that make strategic sense?

Joe Biden

Over the years, I've spent time in Saudi Arabia, the Bekaa Valley, Afghanistan, Jordan, and Kenya, among other vacation hotspots.

Alex Berenson

I would have voted 'no' on the Iraq war and 'yes' to Afghanistan.

Rand Paul

The people who illegally cross into the country are from countries that have very close ties to al Qaeda, whether it's Yemen or Afghanistan, Pakistan, China. It is an absolute national disgrace.

Rick Perry

Afghanistan's borders are arbitrary, drawn to meet 19th-century political needs rather than to respect ethnic or religious patterns.

Stephen Kinzer

As recently as the 1970s, some Pashtun leaders in Afghanistan were pushing to create a new state, Pashtunistan, by joining with Pashtuns in Pakistan.

Stephen Kinzer

Sudan expelled bin Laden on May 18, 1996, to Afghanistan.

Barton Gellman

Afghanistan and Iraq were lumped together in what was called a 'global war on terrorism.'

Richard Engel

Afghanistan was always a backwater in the Islamic world.

Richard Engel

In all the debate about Afghanistan, we don't hear much about our obligation to the wretched lives of Afghan women. They are being treated as collateral damage as the big boys discuss geopolitical goals.

Tina Brown

The women of Afghanistan, left behind as their men fought, did what the women of World War II did - used their wits and resourcefulness to preserve some semblance of civilization.

Tina Brown

As a reporter, I embedded for modest stints with American soldiers in Afghanistan and Iraq. When I'm asked about those experiences, I always say - and mean - that we civilians don't deserve the soldiers we have.

Alex Berenson

I don't want to go and start trying to make jokes in places like India, Tanzania or Iraq. Afghanistan is not a funny place.

Bill Bryson

Because Iran understands Afghanistan far better than Americans do, making Iran a partner in a long-term effort to transform Afghan agriculture makes sense.

Stephen Kinzer

Searches of al Qaeda sites in Afghanistan, undertaken since American-backed forces took control there, are not known to have turned up a significant cache of nuclear materials.

Barton Gellman

Afghanistan does have an air force: It has two C-130s. I saw one of them. It was nice, a gift from the United States. But two planes don't even make a Caribbean charter airline, let alone an air force for a country at war.

Richard Engel

The Syrian border town of Qa'im was the main gateway Islamic radicals used to go to Iraq. Syria became the passageway for extremists from Egypt, Libya, Afghanistan, Yemen, Saudi Arabia and other Muslim nations to fight a jihad against American forces in Iraq.

Richard Engel

Hurtling the Pentagon into an unprecedented budgetary
meltdown is horrifically irresponsible. Obama doesn't care.
This is war - not against the Taliban, but war against the GOP.
He has Republicans on the ropes, and that's a victory he savors
and desires - unlike Afghanistan, where he seems only to want
to turn tail.

John Podhoretz

I didn't know Michael Hastings very well, but one thing about
him was always obvious - he was born to be in the news
business, he loved it, he was made for it. He wrote about Iraq
and Afghanistan as places he had always been destined to visit.

Matt Taibbi

There isn't, even now, a great tradition of novel-writing in
Afghanistan. Most of the literature is in the form of poetry.

Khaled Hosseini

Sacrifice is going to war for your country. Sacrifice is a brave
young man being blown up by a landmine in Afghanistan.

Sebastian Coe

We are particularly interested in the mental health programs and policies that support our troops and their families before, during, and after deployment to Iraq and Afghanistan.

John M. McHugh

Afghanistan is a land-locked country.

Lakhdar Brahimi

A Western-style democracy in Afghanistan is a dream. I don't see that as a reality anytime soon. But I think some form of representative political process is not that far-fetched.

Khaled Hosseini

The United States was an innocent victim after September 11. It had never attacked or occupied Afghanistan. So therefore it had no choice but to go after the aggressors.

Queen Rania of Jordan

You know, if I were an - if I were a Taliban, I'd say, 'What did al-Qaida ever do for me except get me kicked out of Afghanistan?'

Robert M. Gates

If a person is a U.S. citizen, and he is on the battlefield in Afghanistan or Iraq trying to attack our troops, he will face the full brunt of the U.S. military response.

John O. Brennan

The Afghan security forces will always have the help of the U.S. American military to ensure that Afghanistan never fails.

Lindsey Graham

Several million people inside and outside Afghanistan are destitute and desperately in need of help.

Lakhdar Brahimi

To leave Afghanistan as a playground for terrorists and adventurers was simply not possible anymore.

Lakhdar Brahimi

I like to tell people that I have the best job in the media. All I do is hang around with heroes. I do that every week for my 'War Stories' documentary series - and when FOX News wants - I go off and cover the young Americans we send to places like Afghanistan or Iraq.

Oliver North

Look, I think the public generally understands that what's at stake in Afghanistan is American security, number one.

Paul Wolfowitz

You know, I wish the world well. I want Iraq to have democracy and the Haitians to have democracy. I want the people of Afghanistan to thrive. Lord knows, we spend enough money there to help them. What about people at home? Isn't that our first responsibility?

Barbara Boxer

There's no country in the world that's more devastated from natural resources than Afghanistan.

Jim Fowler

We had a couple of minor coups that made a big difference. We snared away from a competitor a correspondent already on the ground in Afghanistan. That was an enormous help to us, because there we were.

Brit Hume

However, it does seem now that the international community, more importantly the powers that have influence, and, even more importantly, Afghanistan's neighbors realize that it is high time that they work together, and not against one another.

Lakhdar Brahimi